DOMINOES

Typhoon

LEVEL TWO 700 HEADWORDS

OXFORD
UNIVERSITY PRESS

Great Clarendon Street, Oxford OX2 6DP

Oxford University Press is a department of the University of Oxford.
It furthers the University's objective of excellence in research, scholarship,
and education by publishing worldwide in

Oxford New York

Auckland Cape Town Dar es Salaam Hong Kong Karachi
Kuala Lumpur Madrid Melbourne Mexico City Nairobi
New Delhi Shanghai Taipei Toronto

With offices in

Argentina Austria Brazil Chile Czech Republic France Greece
Guatemala Hungary Italy Japan Poland Portugal Singapore
South Korea Switzerland Thailand Turkey Ukraine Vietnam

OXFORD and OXFORD ENGLISH are registered trade marks of
Oxford University Press in the UK and in certain other countries

First published in Dominoes 2010

2022

12

ISBN: 978 0 19 424893 8 Book
ISBN: 978 0 19 463970 5 Book and Audio Pack

Printed in China

This book is printed on paper from certified and well-managed sources.

ACKNOWLEDGEMENTS

Cover reproduced with permission from: Alamy Images (ship struggling through storm/
North Wind Picture Archives).

Illustrations by: Emmanuel Cerisier/Beehive Illustration

The publisher would like to thank the following for permission to reproduce photographs: Alamy
Images pp7 (Barometer/Stefan Sollfors), 19 (Typhoon Tokage south of Japan/Stocktrek
Images Inc.); Bridgeman Art Library Ltd p25 (The Mississippi Steam Frigate in a Typhoon,
engraved by Currier & Ives, 1854/The Mariner's Museum, Newport News, Virginia, USA);
Corbis p12 (A ship's log book/DK Limited); Getty Images p31 (old bronze Chinese coins/
David Sanger); iStockphoto p54 (Ancient chinese coin/Ken Pilon); OUP p18 (cloudy sky/
Photodisc); Shutterstock pp24 (rope on ship/Joy Fera), 30 (storm at sea/airn), 39 (ship wheel/
StockPhotosArt), 47 (antique writing desk/Marko Bradic).

DOMINOES

Series Editors: Bill Bowler and Sue Parminter

Typhoon

Joseph Conrad

Text adaptation by Tim Herdon

Illustrated by Emmanuel Cerisier

Joseph Conrad (1857–1924) was born in Poland. By the time he was eleven, both his parents were dead, and in 1874 Conrad moved to France, and later to England, and began working as a sailor. Nearly twenty years at sea gave him ideas for many of his novels. He chose to write in English, and his first novel, *Almayer's Folly*, was published in 1894. The same year, at thirty-seven years old, and after many love affairs, Conrad married an English woman sixteen years younger than himself. His novels *Typhoon* (1902) and *The Secret Agent* (1907) are both available as *Dominoes*.

OXFORD
UNIVERSITY PRESS

ACTIVITIES

BEFORE READING

1 What is a typhoon? Choose one of the following. Use a dictionary to help you.

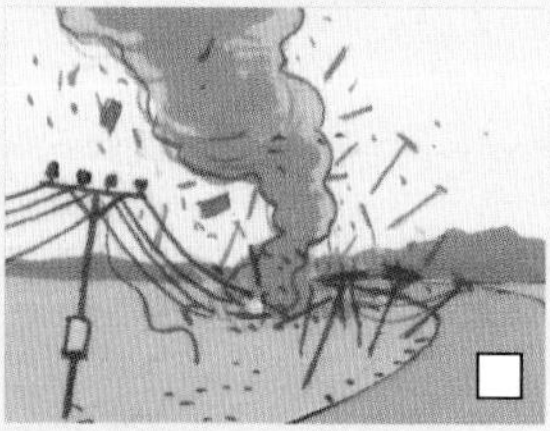

a a strong wind that moves very fast in a circle

b a strong tropical storm near China or India

c big waves that are many metres high when they hit beaches

2 The ship in the story *Typhoon* is a steamship. Which kind of ship is this? Choose.

3 Here are some of the people in *Typhoon*. Match the sentences with the pictures.

1 Mr Solomon Rout

2 Lucy MacWhirr

3 Captain MacWhirr

4 Mrs Rout

5 The boatswain

6 Mr Jukes

a ☐ He's the most important man on the ship, and he speaks very little.

b ☐ He's the second most important man on the ship, and he's young.

c ☐ He's worked on ships for many years, and he knows a lot about them.

d ☐ He's not a very clever man, and he's always smiling.

e ☐ She's the captain's wife, and she's not very interested in him.

f ☐ She's Solomon Rout's wife, and she looks after his mother.

CHAPTER 1 Captain MacWhirr

'There's some bad weather out there,' **Captain** MacWhirr said to himself, looking at the **barometer**.

He was a quiet man, who never looked for trouble, and rarely found it. When he talked, which was not often, he used few words. This made some people think that he was not so clever. He had blue eyes, not much hair on top of his head – with thin yellow hair around the back and sides, and thick red hair on his face. He had a strong, thick, short body. **On shore** – it didn't matter where – he always wore the same brown hat, brown suit, and heavy black **boots**. But everyone who worked with him knew that he was a good captain. Ships under his **command** arrived on time, and he never had trouble with his **crews**.

When he was fifteen, MacWhirr ran away from home in Ireland to be a sailor. He didn't tell his mother and father – who had a shop in Belfast – where he was until eight months later, when he sent them a letter from Chile. Year after year he worked on different ships, and didn't go home very often. But he wrote many letters home from all over the world. They were short, and always gave news about the weather: 'It's very hot here' or 'On Christmas Day at four o'clock in the afternoon it was very cold.'

captain the most important person on a ship

barometer this shows you how the weather is changing

on shore on the ground, not at sea

boots long shoes that cover the feet and the bottom of the legs

command when you are the person who decides what happens in a place you have this

crew the people who work on a ship

In time he met a young woman that he liked. Her name was Lucy, but he did not have time to write much about her to his mother and father, because they died. MacWhirr married Lucy not long after he was given his first job as the captain of a ship.

The *Nan-Shan* was three years old and was made in Dumbarton, in Scotland. She was a fine, strong ship, neither too narrow nor too deep, and good in stormy weather. At first the *Nan-Shan* sailed under a British **flag**, but then the owner, Mr Sigg, decided that it would be better to change to the old Thai flag. This was red with a big, white **elephant** in the middle of it. Jukes, the **first mate**, felt uncomfortable sailing under Thai colours.

flag a piece of cloth with colours on it; you put this on a ship to show which country it belongs to

elephant a very big animal with a long nose

first mate one of the most important people on a ship after the captain

'It looks strange to me, that flag with the elephant on it,' he said to Captain MacWhirr. 'I don't like it.'

'There's nothing wrong with it,' replied Captain MacWhirr, looking up at the flag. 'You just have to make sure that the crew put it the right way up.'

Jukes wasn't happy with the captain's answer. Later, down on **deck**, he told Solomon Rout about it. Rout, taking time out from the **engine** room, was the **chief** engineer. He was a tall, fatherly man, and often listened – smiling – to young Jukes's stories.

'I can't understand the captain,' said Jukes. 'You say one thing to him, and he takes it another way. I was ready to leave my job because we're now sailing under that Thai flag. But all he could say was that you had to put it up the right way.'

'And *did* you leave your job?' asked Rout, smiling. After many years' work on ships all over the world, Rout knew how important it was to have – and not to lose – a good job.

'No, I didn't,' replied Jukes. He felt a little angry with himself because he talked of it but didn't do it.

'Rout!' said the captain, arriving just then.

'Yes, sir!' Rout replied.

'We're sailing for Fu-chau this afternoon. The engines must be ready for one o'clock. And Jukes!'

'Yes, sir?'

'We're taking two hundred Chinese **labourers** with us. They're arriving in about twenty minutes. During the day they can stay on deck, and at night they'll sleep in the **hold**. Make sure that there's room for them and their boxes.'

deck where you walk outside on a ship

engine the machine in a ship that makes it move

chief the most important one, who tells others what to do

labourer someone strong who does hard work for little money

hold the big room inside a ship where you put things during a sea journey

'Yes, sir,' said Jukes. And with that the captain went to his room, and Rout and Jukes hurried away to do their work.

The two hundred Chinese workers were going back to their villages after seven years of work away from home. They all wore the same dark clothes, and each one carried a little box which was made of wood. In this box was everything that they had in the world, and all their work money. Each one kept his box near him at all times. When they came onto the *Nan-Shan*, Jukes told them where to go. Because the Chinese labourers couldn't speak English very well, he explained everything very loudly and slowly to them: 'You sleep here. You cook food here, and here you eat. In fine weather, you can come up, walk on deck, and enjoy the sea air.' Did the Chinese workers understand him? Their tired faces didn't show what they were really thinking, so it was difficult to be sure.

In four hours the ship would leave for Fu-chau. There was just time to write to family and friends, and MacWhirr, Rout and Jukes all wanted to send letters before leaving.

MacWhirr's letter was to his wife. Spending so much time at sea, Captain MacWhirr didn't understand his wife and their two children – Lydia and Tom – very well. He knew little about their lives, and had little to tell them about his life. Lucy MacWhirr usually didn't read her husband's letters very carefully: they spoke about the weather, the sea, and other things that she didn't really find very interesting. Her one great worry was that one day he would come back, and want to live at home with her all the time. So she read his letters looking for any words about that. *Remember me to the children. Your loving husband,* wrote MacWhirr, before he put his name at the bottom.

Rout's letters were much fuller, and his wife always enjoyed reading them. She lived with Rout's mother, who couldn't hear very well, and needed help. And she often read the really interesting parts of her husband's letters very loudly to the old woman. *I prefer a slow captain who does no wrong to a quick-thinking criminal one. They're easier to work with,* wrote Rout to his wife, thinking of MacWhirr.

Jukes always wrote to a friend of his – a sailor on another ship – and he usually described everything that happened in his life, and how he thought and felt about it. In this letter he wrote: *The other day I was talking with one of the crew for a while, and later the captain asked me: 'Was that you talking?' I said, 'Yes.' 'For two hours!' he said. 'What do you find to talk about? When we're on shore I see people talking all day, and then in the evening they go on talking over drinks. Surely they're saying the same things over again. I can't understand it.' Isn't he a strange man? Sometimes he makes me angry, and sometimes I feel sorry for him – because I think that he doesn't really understand anything of life at all.*

After the three writers finished and posted their letters, the *Nan-Shan* was ready to go on her way.

READING CHECK

Are these sentences true or false? Tick the boxes.

	True	False
a MacWhirr is a man who doesn't like trouble.	☑	☐
b From the age of fifteen, MacWhirr saw little of his parents.	☐	☐
c The *Nan-Shan* usually sails around the coast of Scotland.	☐	☐
d The *Nan-Shan* is taking some Chinese workers back to their homes.	☐	☐
e Jukes agrees with MacWhirr about the Thai flag.	☐	☐
f Solomon Rout writes long letters to his wife.	☐	☐
g MacWhirr understands his wife and children very well.	☐	☐
h MacWhirr talks a lot.	☐	☐
i Jukes doesn't think that MacWhirr is a very clever man.	☐	☐

WORD WORK

1 Put these people on the ship in the correct order, from the most important (1) to the least important (4).

2 Complete the sentences with other new words from Chapter 1 in the correct form.

a Captain MacWhirr looks at the barometer and sees on it that the weather is changing.

b There's something wrong with the ship's ....; we're going slower and slower.

c Normally you can see which country a ship is from if you look up at its ....

d The crew will have two days' rest .... before the ship sails for Fu-chau.

e If you're feeling sick down here, you can go for a walk up on ....

f He had problems taking his small .... off his big feet.

g The Chinese labourers have to sleep down in the .... of the ship.

h After the captain, the next person in .... of the ship is the first mate.

i A white .... was a very special animal in Thailand. Important people often gave them as presents.

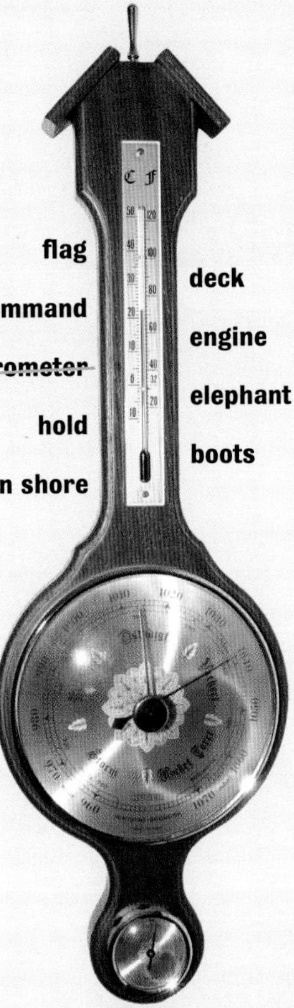

GUESS WHAT

What happens in the next chapter? Tick four boxes.

a The Chinese labourers say that they don't want to sleep in the hold. ☐

b The weather gets worse. ☐

c The weather gets better. ☐

d Captain MacWhirr is worried about bad weather. ☐

e Captain MacWhirr isn't worried about bad weather. ☐

f The *Nan-Shan* starts the journey to Fu-chau. ☐

g Jukes says that he can't work on a ship with a Thai flag. ☐

h Jukes shows the Chinese labourers where they must stay during the journey. ☐

CHAPTER 2 Things get hotter

Once the *Nan-Shan* was out at sea, Captain MacWhirr looked at the barometer again. 'Yes, there's some really dirty weather out there, that's for sure,' he said to himself.

idea something that you think

He was not worried by the way the weather was changing, and he didn't feel at all afraid at the **idea** of a typhoon. Spending most of his life at sea, he knew many different kinds of weather; and a typhoon was just another kind of bad weather for him. But perhaps Captain MacWhirr did not fully know the real

power of the sea. Of course he knew about typhoons, and he knew that they sometimes happened in the China Sea. Before becoming a captain, he read about typhoons in books, and he heard about them from other sailors. But to be in the middle of a very strong typhoon in which the sea showed all its **fury** and its terrible power – no, this was something that MacWhirr himself did not really know.

The **swell** was getting stronger, and the ship started **rolling** slowly and heavily from side to side. It was now late afternoon, and the sun was beginning to go down. It was very hot, there was no wind at all, and MacWhirr could feel the storm in the air. Perhaps everyone on the *Nan-Shan* could feel it, because there was a heavy, angry feeling everywhere on the ship. Most of the Chinese labourers were on deck, spending the time in different ways. Some were looking out to sea, bored. Some were smoking, and some had their shirts off and were pulling up **buckets** full of sea water from over the side of the ship to wash in because they were so hot. Three of them were **pointing** at one of their boxes and shouting. Perhaps they were talking angrily about money, thought MacWhirr. The rest of them were sleeping quietly.

Below deck, it was worse. The temperature in the engine room was a hundred and seventeen **degrees**, and the air was full of angry voices and the loud noise of **metal** on metal. The second engineer, a big, strong man called Harry, was shouting at his men because there was not **enough steam**. Harry often shouted, and usually the men worked quietly

power when something or someone is strong they have this; when you can do something

fury what you feel when you are very angry

swell the way that the sea moves up and down

roll to move from side to side

bucket you can carry water in this

point to show something with a finger or hand; to be turned one way

degree we use this to measure how hot or cold something is, or which way a ship is travelling across the sea

metal iron is a cheap metal; most of a modern ship is made of this

enough as much of something or as many things as you need

steam you see this white cloud in the air when water is very hot; it made old trains' and ships' engines work

under him; but today they were as angry as he was. To make more steam, they needed more air from the **ventilators** – and there was none. Harry came up on deck to see why this was, and found Jukes.

'How can my men give us enough steam if the ventilators aren't catching the wind?' he shouted.

'The ventilators aren't the problem,' said Jukes. 'There's *no* wind – that's the problem.' Jukes knew that it was hard work in the engine room on a day like this, and so he decided it would be a good idea to **let** Harry shout for a while. Perhaps after that, he would go back down below deck and do his job more quietly. But the second engineer didn't listen to Jukes's words.

'Look, it's just like I thought. This ventilator's pointing in the wrong **direction**. I don't know what your men do all day. Do they just lie around on their fat backs?' He tried to change the direction of the ventilator, but it was too heavy to move. Jukes stopped him: 'Harry, I told you before: there's nothing that we can do. There's no wind. But look, there's a storm coming.' Harry looked at the

ventilators they take air down to the engine room

let not to stop

direction the way that someone or something goes

strong swell of the sea around them, and then at Jukes. 'This is a dog's life,' he said, angrily. And with that, he went back down to the engine room.

Jukes turned round, and saw MacWhirr looking at him.

'Why did you let him talk to you like that?' the captain asked. 'You mustn't be soft with the crew. If he goes on like that, he'll have to find himself a new job on another ship very soon.'

'His men can't make enough steam. And it's not easy working down there when it's so hot, I understand how he feels. Even up here on deck I feel like I have a **blanket** round my head.'

'A blanket round your head? What *do* you mean? Have you ever had a blanket round your head, Jukes? What was that for?'

'It's just a way of speaking, sir,' said Jukes, thinking that Captain MacWhirr really had a very strange way of understanding things.

'Well, if there's any more talk of that kind from the second engineer, he'll have to go,' said MacWhirr, and he walked away.

At eight o'clock it was dark. Jukes went to the **chart-room** to write the ship's **log**. As he did every day, he wrote the number of miles, the direction the ship was sailing in, and what kind of wind there was that day. Should he write down what he thought, or only what he could see? Under '**Comments**' he wrote: *'Terribly hot weather,'* and: *'The swell is making the ship roll heavily.'* He thought for one or two minutes, and then wrote: *'The Chinese labourers are all safely below deck for the night. The barometer is still going down.'* He was closing the log, when the ship rolled very heavily. He looked out of the window. In front of his eyes a great big dark **wave** climbed up higher and higher until it hid the starry sky. He wrote one more comment in the log: *'From what I can see, a typhoon is on its way.'*

blanket something that you put on the bed to stay warm at night

chart-room the room on a ship where the captain makes plans for which way the ship should go

log a ship's diary

comment a thing to say

wave a line of water that moves across the top of the sea

ACTIVITIES

READING CHECK

Put these sentences in the correct order from 1–7.

a Jukes tells Harry that there is no wind. ☐
b An enormous wave hides the stars. ☐
c The ship starts to roll from side to side. ☐
d MacWhirr tells Jukes that he shouldn't let Harry shout at him. ☐
e Jukes writes in the ship's log that he thinks there will be a typhoon. ☐
f Harry comes on deck to see why the ventilators are not working. ☐
g MacWhirr looks at the barometer. [1]

WORD WORK

1 Make seven more new words from Chapter 2 using this circle of letters. (You can use the letters as many times as you need.)

L O G
R _ _ _
W _ _ _
P _ _ _ _
S _ _ _ _
S _ _ _ _
M _ _ _ _
L _ _

2 Use words from Activity 1 in the correct form to complete the sentences.

a The captain writes important things in the ship's ...log... every day.
b The *Nan-Shan* is made of .... and wood.
c Look at that ship! It's .... from side to side in the sea.

d The *Titanic* was a big old .... ship.

e Will you .... me do something? You're so busy and I want to help!

f Big green .... are hitting the side of the ship and pushing her onto the rocks.

g The engine doesn't have any .... today. What's wrong?

h The weather is bad and the .... around us is getting worse and worse.

3 Unscramble the words from Chapter 2 to complete these sentences.

a Which ..direction.. is London from here? Is it north-west or north-east? (nirotecid)

b Does anybody have any .... to make on what I've just said? Please speak up. (scotnemm)

c I need some more water. I'm very thirsty, and this small bottle isn't .... for me. (nugeoh)

d The captain is in the ...., looking at the maps. (tarch-moor)

e It's so hot here out in the sun; it must be at least forty .... (desgeer)

f It's a cold night tonight. I've put a second .... on your bed to keep you warm. (laktenb)

g He was full of .... when a car suddenly drove out in front of him. (rufy)

h When you're on holiday in a different country and can't speak the language, use a finger to .... to things that you want to buy. (tinop)

i Can you bring me a .... of water? My horse is thirsty. (cubtek)

GUESS WHAT

What happens next? Tick the boxes.	**Yes**	**No**
a The weather calms down.	☐	☐
b Jukes and MacWhirr have a talk about the weather.	☐	☐
c The crew in the engine room start fighting.	☐	☐
d MacWhirr tells the engineer that he will have to leave the ship in Fu-chau.	☐	☐
e They sail into a storm.	☐	☐
f They change direction to avoid a storm.	☐	☐
g MacWhirr decides to sail the ship back to port.	☐	☐

CHAPTER 3 The book of storms

After Jukes finished writing his comments in the log book, the captain arrived in the chart-room, and it was Jukes's turn to go below deck. Out on the **bridge**, he met the second mate – a strange man with bad teeth, a long nose, and a red, angry-looking face. He never spoke much to the rest of the crew. This was his first trip on the *Nan-Shan*.

'It's a good thing for those Chinese labourers that this ship doesn't roll so easily in a storm,' said Jukes laughing brightly, 'don't you think?'

'Just you wait,' said the second mate.

'Do you mean to say that it's going to get worse?' asked Jukes.

'You said it. Not me!' said the second mate with a cold smile.

The ship was rolling more wildly now than before, and in the end Jukes decided that he must go back and speak to Captain MacWhirr. It was a stupid idea to sail the ship into a typhoon. They should try and do something about it. Back once more in the chart-room, he found MacWhirr reading a book there.

'What's the matter?' asked MacWhirr.

'The swell's getting worse, sir,' replied Jukes.

'Yes, I can see that,' said MacWhirr. 'Anything else?'

Jukes was not sure how to begin. Then he had an idea.

'I was thinking of the passengers, sir.'

'What passengers, Jukes?'

'The Chinese labourers, sir.'

'Well, why don't you say what you mean? I've never heard anyone talk of Chinese labourers as paying passengers before! Ha! That's a good one!' he laughed. 'And what about them?' he went on.

'Well, with all this rolling, a lot of water is coming into the

bridge the part of a ship where the captain and other important sailors stand and tell others what to do

ship's hold. That's where all the Chinese are, sir. I thought that maybe we could go east. Then the swell would come at us straight on, and not make us roll from side to side.'

'So you want me to move a powerful steamship fifty degrees **off course** to make some Chinese labourers more comfortable? I've heard some stupid things in my life, but this ... And what do you want us to do after that? Go fifty degrees the other way again to finish up back **on course**?'

'I know that you don't think much of my idea, sir, but at the moment we're busy sailing into a typhoon,' said Jukes, looking MacWhirr in the eye.

'And it **seems** you think that we should try and sail away from it?'

Jukes said nothing. This was a different Captain MacWhirr from the one he knew. MacWhirr held up the book in his hand.

off course going in the wrong direction

on course going in the right direction

seem to look like

'I was just reading the chapter on storms in this book. I think you'd like it. If we do what it says in this book, we have to sail all over the sea trying to **avoid** storms. Can you believe that? Think of us sailing an **extra** three hundred miles on our way to Fu-chau, just because of bad weather. What about the extra **coal** – the extra time? Think of us coming into Fu-chau two days late; what will they say to me? *"Where have you been, Captain?"* "Oh, it took us longer: we had to avoid some bad weather," I'll say. Then they'll ask: *"Was it a very bad storm?"* "I don't know," I'll have to answer. "I didn't see it".'

The captain looked at Jukes. Did the first mate understand what he was saying? MacWhirr tried to explain more:

'That kind of thinking is all wrong, Jukes. A storm is a storm, and a steamship has just got to go through the storms that stand in front of her as well as she can. There are some things that books can't tell you.' MacWhirr stopped talking, and sat down on the window seat. He pulled off his boots and put his legs up. He suddenly felt tired.

'Jukes, tell them to call me if there's any change in the weather.'

'Yes, sir,' answered the first mate, and – with that – he walked out on deck again, closing the chart-room door behind him.

Captain MacWhirr closed his eyes. He was tired after all that speaking. Those twenty minutes of conversation with Jukes were all that he believed about the sea and sailing. Now his head felt empty, and he could think of nothing.

He opened his eyes some time later. What was that loud noise? Was it the wind? Why did no one call him? Just then, he saw Jukes's face at the open chart-room door. The first mate was shouting something, but the captain couldn't hear him very well because of the wind.

avoid to move away from or round something

extra more than usual

coal it is hard and black and burns very well; people use it to make the fire that moves old trains and ships

'Started ... this suddenly ... five minutes ago,' cried Jukes.

MacWhirr tried to put on his boots. This was not easy because the ship was now moving from side to side very wildly. At last they were on.

Through the wind Jukes heard the captain saying: 'I told you ... any change ... call me.'

Jukes tried to explain: 'Wind ... sudden ... north-east ... thought you ... sure ... hear.' Again the wind carried away half his words before the captain's ears could catch them.

'We must try to stay on course for as long as we can,' said MacWhirr.

Suddenly the *Nan-Shan* went up over an **enormous** wave, and ran deep down into the sea on the other side of it. Water flew over her sides. Jukes and MacWhirr couldn't see anything for some minutes. When they could see again, Jukes pulled at MacWhirr's arm, and pointed up over their heads. Just then, all the stars went suddenly from before their eyes, and all that they could see was a heavy, coal-dark sky above them.

enormous very big

READING CHECK

Match the two halves of each sentence.

a Jukes asks MacWhirr to
b MacWhirr is reading a book
c Jukes says that
d MacWhirr says that a steamship must
e MacWhirr tells Jukes that
f MacWhirr has a short rest
g The storm starts
h MacWhirr finds it difficult to

1 put on his boots.
2 a lot of water will go in the hold.
3 change course.
4 because he is tired.
5 going off course isn't a good thing to do.
6 about storms.
7 go through any storms that it meets.
8 very suddenly.

WORD WORK

Find the words in the clouds to complete the sentences.

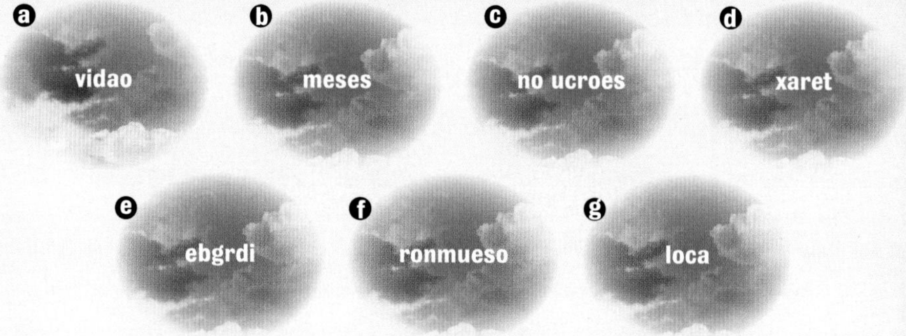

a If you want to go into London, you should ....avoid.... going by car. It's easier by train.
b He .... really nice to me. How did you meet him?
c Try to keep the boat .... We're going too far east.
d We really loved Beijing and so we decided to stay two .... days there.
e The captain is standing on the ...., looking at the weather.
f You've caught a really big one! I think it's the most .... fish that I've ever seen.
g Put some more .... on the fire. This room's really cold.

GUESS WHAT

What happens in the next chapter? Match the two halves of each sentence.

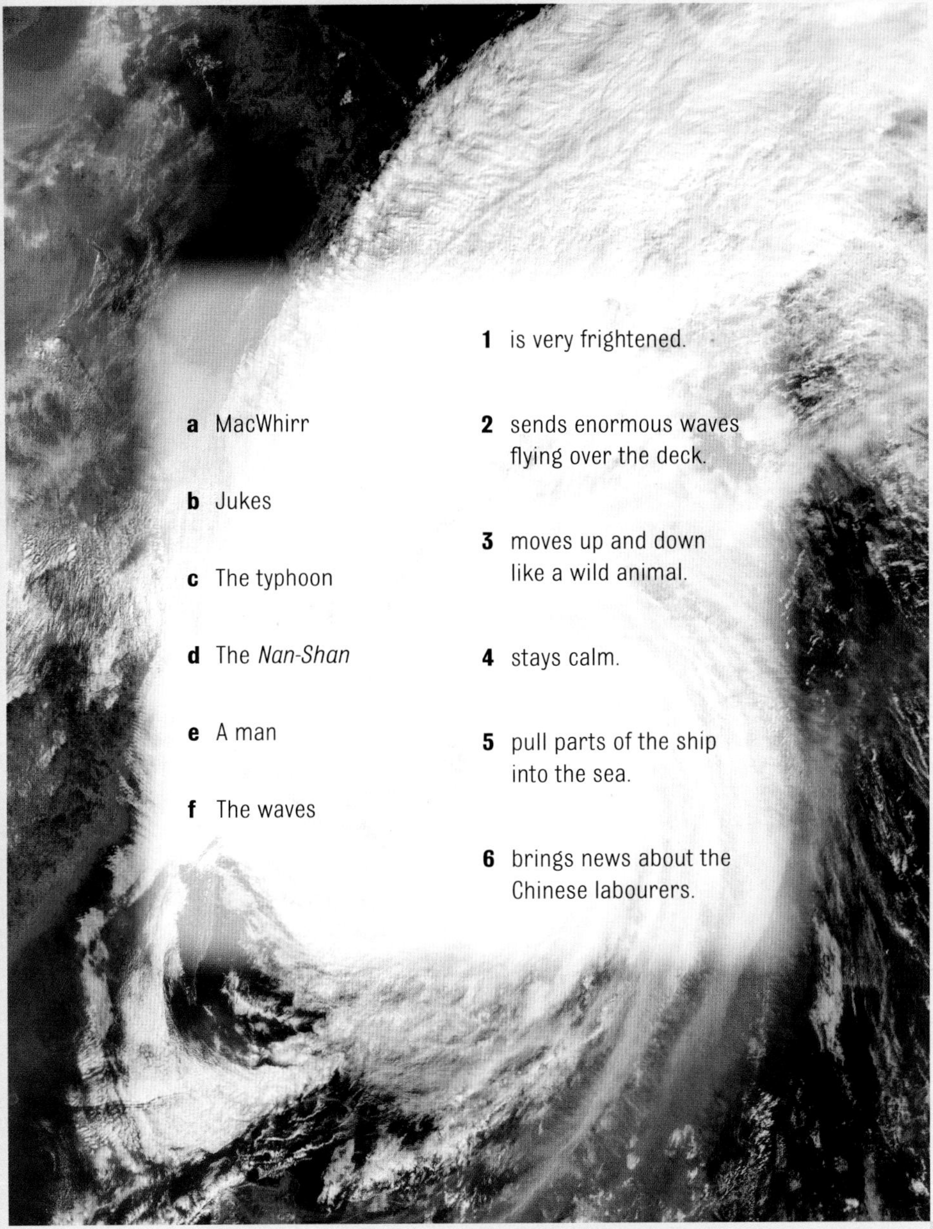

a MacWhirr
b Jukes
c The typhoon
d The *Nan-Shan*
e A man
f The waves

1 is very frightened.
2 sends enormous waves flying over the deck.
3 moves up and down like a wild animal.
4 stays calm.
5 pull parts of the ship into the sea.
6 brings news about the Chinese labourers.

CHAPTER 4 The typhoon hits

fasten to stop something moving around

fear the feeling that you have when you are afraid

Jukes knew that at a time like this, a ship's officer must not show his feelings. He started to tell his men to **fasten** anything on the ship that was moving. He wanted them to see in him a man who was not afraid of some bad weather, a man who knew that this typhoon was coming from the beginning. But with every minute, Jukes understood that this typhoon was much bigger, and wilder, than any other usual storm. Great waves fell noisily onto the deck, covering the *Nan-Shan* in water from top to bottom. She was still rolling heavily from side to side, but now she began to move up and down wildly in the sea, too, like an enormous animal worried sick with **fear**.

'I'm not sure that we're going to live through this,' thought Jukes. He felt happy that Captain MacWhirr was there, for it was the captain who had to decide

what to do in difficult times. And saving the crew's lives was the captain's job, not his.

MacWhirr did not feel so comfortable. He knew that he and his crew could all die in this typhoon, and he knew that he must decide what to do very carefully. It was now a question of life or death. He looked in front of him, trying to understand how the typhoon worked, like a man looking deeply into the eyes of a dangerous enemy. But all was dark around him. He could see nothing, not even the ship under his feet. He felt like a man who has lost the power to see, and who doesn't know where he is.

Standing next to him, Jukes said: 'I think that we've sailed into the worst **part** of the typhoon.' But this was not true: the worst part came a few minutes later, and it came suddenly. The typhoon exploded around them with dangerous power. It seemed that the wind and the waves wanted to break the ship into hundreds of pieces. Many sailors tried to **grab** some part of the ship, but couldn't do it in time. The waves sent them flying down the deck. Jukes was thrown onto his back. It seemed to him that all of the China Sea was trying to **drown** him. It threw him wildly from side to side, and he heard himself shouting, again and again: 'My God! My God! My God!' Hurrying to find something to hold on to, his hands touched a boot, then two boots. He held on, and then he felt Captain MacWhirr's strong arms around him, pulling him up. They stood for a short while, holding onto each other, but then the water knocked them onto the deck. At last they found each other again, and this time they held on to the ship's **railings**.

The typhoon was now pulling the **lifeboats** off the ship. One by one, they went into the angry waters of the China Sea.

'Our lifeboats have gone, sir,' shouted Jukes. Because of the noise of the wind he couldn't hear MacWhirr's answer very well:

'Can't help ... had to happen ... some things ... left behind.'

part some, but not all, of something

grab to take someone or something quickly in your hands

drown to die in water

railing a metal thing that stops you falling from somewhere high

lifeboat you use this boat to get away if your ship starts going down in the sea

survive to live through a difficult or dangerous time

The captain's words surprised Jukes. Was that all that MacWhirr had to say? Again, he found the Captain's way of thinking strange. The first mate looked at the waves loudly hitting the deck, and tried to decide if the *Nan-Shan* would **survive** the typhoon. If the engines kept going ... if the waves didn't break the deck ... if not too much water went into the hold ... But then he thought, more or less without fear: 'No, she won't survive.'

At the same time that he was thinking this, he felt Captain MacWhirr's heavy arm over his shoulder. He replied by putting his own arm round MacWhirr.

'Will she live through this?' he asked the captain. At first there was no answer, only the angry noise of the wind and the sea against the ship's side. But then he heard MacWhirr's voice: 'Going to ... all right ... good ship ... everything will ... for the best.' Jukes wasn't sure if this was more of the captain's slow but

sure way of thinking, or if the ship really would be all right. But it was good to hear MacWhirr's words.

'Where are ... crew?' asked Macwhirr.

'What ... say, sir?' Jukes couldn't hear his question.

'Where ... all the men?' said MacWhirr.

Just then Jukes felt a hand touching his boot, then a second hand, and then he felt both these hands pulling on his trousers. A man was on his knees, trying to stand up. He was using Jukes's body to help him. It was the **boatswain**. He was a little man, with short legs and long arms, who usually smiled a lot.

'Is that you, sir?' he said to MacWhirr.

'Yes, boatswain. What have you come to tell us?' replied MacWhirr.

'It's about the Chinese labourers, sir.'

'Well, what about them, boatswain?' said Jukes.

'The sea has taken them all, sir.'

boatswain /'bəʊsn/ the most important person on a ship after the captain and the two mates

ACTIVITIES

READING CHECK

Correct seven more mistakes in the chapter summary.

The storm gets ~~better~~ worse and the ship begins to move wildly. Jukes knows that he must be calm, but it is easy. He has often been in storms like this before. The strong waves make him fall down, and he has to grab MacWhirr's ears. MacWhirr puts his arm around Jukes's shoulders, and Jukes feels worse. MacWhirr tells him not to worry, and that everything is going to be all wrong. But then the boatswain comes and tells them some good news: all the Japanese labourers in the hold have fallen into the sea, he says.

WORD WORK

Complete the sentences with the correct form of the words in the rope.

a He ..drowned.. when he fell into the sea because he didn't know how to swim.

b Please ask for the bread, don't just put out your hand and .... it.

c Here is .... of the money that I borrowed from you. I'll give you the rest tomorrow.

d Everyone must .... their seat belts before the plane takes off.

e Hold on to the .... at the top of the stairs carefully: it's a long way to fall.

f .... is our greatest enemy. When we are afraid, we don't do things we want to, or need to do.

g When the *Titanic* started going down, they found that there weren't enough .... for everybody on the ship.

h Fewer than half the passengers .... the accident; all the rest died.

GUESS WHAT

What happens in the next chapter? Tick four boxes.

- **a** The boatswain tells MacWhirr and Jukes what he saw. ☐
- **b** Jukes thinks the boatswain is good at his job. ☐
- **c** MacWhirr thinks the boatswain is good at his job. ☐
- **d** The Chinese labourers are safe from the typhoon in the hold. ☐
- **e** The Chinese labourers are playing cards in the hold. ☐
- **f** The Chinese labourers are terrified of the typhoon. ☐
- **g** Because lots of water gets into the hold, the Chinese labourers drown. ☐
- **h** MacWhirr sends Jukes to the hold to see what has really happened there. ☐

CHAPTER 5 We need light

'What do you mean, the sea has taken all the Chinese labourers?' MacWhirr asked the boatswain.

'I saw an enormous wave ... it took them all, together in one big group.'

'Are you sure about that, boatswain?' Jukes asked. He didn't think the boatswain was very clever. He never understood why Captain MacWhirr believed that he was good at his job.

'I saw it happen with my own two eyes, sir,' said the boatswain. He then told them everything that happened from the time that the typhoon struck:

When the boatswain and the rest of the crew saw that they were in a typhoon, they ran from the deck, and looked for somewhere drier to escape from the worst of the storm. Many of them went to a dark room under the bridge. Here, the ship rolled as much as it did on deck, but there was less water. It was very dark, and the crew were in the middle of a typhoon for the first time. Most thought that it would be their last time too. Fear made them start shouting, and with every wave that hit the deck, their shouts became louder. One of them said that they needed a light. If the ship was going to **sink**, at least they could see around them before they died.

'I don't like the idea of drowning in the dark,' he said.

'Well, if you want a light so badly, why don't you get one yourself?' answered the boatswain. This made them shout even more, for not one of them wanted to go out into the storm. The boatswain didn't want to go and look for a light either: outside the room that they were in, anything could happen. And the nearest place to find lights was far away. But then he

sink when a ship goes down under the water and doesn't come up again

remembered that there were six lights in the hold, where all the Chinese labourers were. He decided to go to the hold and bring one back.

Outside, the ship was rolling wildly from side to side. The wind, the powerful waves hitting the deck all around him, the moving ship – all seemed to be doing their best to kill him. With every step that he took, he was afraid that he would fall **overboard** into the angry China Sea below him. He fought his way to the hold, falling many times. The typhoon was breaking the ship into pieces, and he often had to avoid pieces of thin metal that the sea and the wind threw at him. The noise of the typhoon was terrible to hear. The wind was screaming at him: it was a noise halfway between fury and **pain**. But underneath the screaming wind, and the noise of metal hitting metal, there was something strange and new that he could hear: a deep **thumping** noise. Was it coming from the hold? It seemed that something very large and heavy was rolling from one side of the ship to the other. The boatswain couldn't understand it – there was nothing large and heavy in the hold that could make that noise. But as he came closer to the hold, the thumping noise became louder and louder.

overboard off the ship and in the sea

pain the feeling that you have in your body when you are hurt

thumping a low banging

pile a number of things one on top of the other

At last he arrived at the heavy metal door to the hold, and pulled it slowly open. What he found inside was terrible to see. The typhoon was throwing the Chinese labourers from one side of the hold to the other. There was nothing for them to hold onto, so they could not stop themselves. When each new wave hit the ship, they rolled into a big **pile** on one side; then they all rolled back into a big pile on the other side. The hold was full of their shouts and screams.

The boatswain also saw many little pieces of

wood all around the hold, together with many round pieces of bright metal. Suddenly he remembered the labourers' boxes: now they were all in pieces, and the money that was once inside them was falling all over the hold. It was like a great storm inside the ship, but a stormy sea of arms, legs, and **terrified** faces – not of wind and waves. And so it was that the sea took them!

Forgetting the lights, which were why he went on his journey to the hold in the first place, the boatswain hurried out of the room and closed the heavy door behind him quickly. He had to tell the captain about this! Crossing the deck, which had sea water all over it, he thought a number of times that the ship was sinking. There were no **ladders** up to the bridge now, but he half rode the waves and half climbed up to the **wheelhouse**. Outside he found the second mate, lying by the door.

'Where's the captain?' asked the boatswain.

'Overboard, like the first mate, and like we'll all be soon,' said the second mate, laughing strangely.

On his hands and knees, the boatswain moved along the bridge away from the man, and it was then that he found Jukes and the captain.

After MacWhirr heard the boatswain's words, he was silent for a while. He asked himself what was really happening down in the hold. Were the Chinese labourers on the ship, fighting, or in the sea, drowning? After thinking about it for some time, he turned to Jukes.

'You must go down to the hold with the boatswain. If those Chinese labourers are fighting over their money, you'll have to stop them. But be careful. If anything happens to me, the ship will be under your command. See what's happened down there, and then use the **speaking-tube** in the engine room to tell me.'

terrified very afraid

ladder you use this for climbing up or down tall buildings or other things

wheelhouse the room where you use a wheel to change the direction of the ship

speaking-tube something that you use for talking to people in another part of the ship

ACTIVITIES

READING CHECK

Circle the correct words to complete the sentences.

a MacWhirr and Jukes listen to the *boatswain's* / *second mate's* story.
b The boatswain goes to find lights for the *Chinese labourers* / *crew*.
c They are in a dark room under the *bridge* / *hold*.
d The boatswain hears a thumping noise coming from the *engine room* / *hold*.
e The boatswain sees *money* / *stones* on the deck.
f The second mate says that *Rout* / *MacWhirr* has gone overboard.
g MacWhirr sends *Rout* / *Jukes* to see the Chinese labourers.
h MacWhirr tells Jukes to use the speaking-tube in the *engine room* / *hold*.

WORD WORK

1 Find six more words from Chapter 5 in the wordsquare.

S	E	P	A	I	N	N	S	V	H	L	L
P	T	E	R	R	I	F	I	E	D	Y	Q
E	X	Y	G	Z	G	N	K	N	S	P	P
A	R	U	O	V	E	R	B	O	A	R	D
K	L	T	H	U	M	P	I	N	G	J	D
I	P	K	O	P	I	B	S	J	X	B	O
N	F	Z	A	Q	R	H	I	O	X	O	E
G	Q	O	E	T	V	X	K	W	S	T	P
T	C	O	N	H	O	S	Z	Y	W	T	I
U	K	P	D	P	A	I	A	I	X	Y	L
B	N	P	G	U	X	N	M	X	F	R	E
E	N	K	W	E	L	K	S	C	M	B	O

2 Complete the sentences with the correct form of the words from Activity 1.

a You can use the .....speaking-tube..... to talk from up here to the chief engineer down in the engine room.

b The .... in my leg is terrible. I think my ankle's broken. It really hurts.

c We heard a strange .... noise coming from the bedroom upstairs. The children were jumping on their beds.

d Put all your dirty clothes in a .... on the chair over there. I'll wash them later.

e Quick! There's a man .... He can't swim so we must save him!

f Get into the lifeboats now; the ship is .... and will soon be under the water.

g He doesn't like aeroplanes; he feels .... when he flies.

GUESS WHAT

What happens next? Tick the boxes.

	Yes	No
a Jukes doesn't want to go down to the hold.	☐	☐
b Jukes thinks that they won't survive the typhoon.	☐	☐
c The Chinese labourers are all fighting over their money.	☐	☐
d The Chinese labourers are trying to get out of the hold.	☐	☐
e MacWhirr tries to change course.	☐	☐
f The boatswain goes overboard.	☐	☐
g The storm is still bad.	☐	☐
h The engines stop working.	☐	☐

CHAPTER 6 The fight to survive

numb not feeling anything

When the worst part of the typhoon started, Jukes stood still, and just held strongly onto the railing in front of him. He tried not to think about what would happen, about the danger that they were in. As the typhoon got worse, he stopped feeling the water and the wind on his face. He was cold and wet all over his body. His arms and legs began to feel **numb**, and his thoughts came slowly. In some ways it was a good feeling. He didn't hope to survive, because hoping meant fighting for something. He couldn't fight any more.

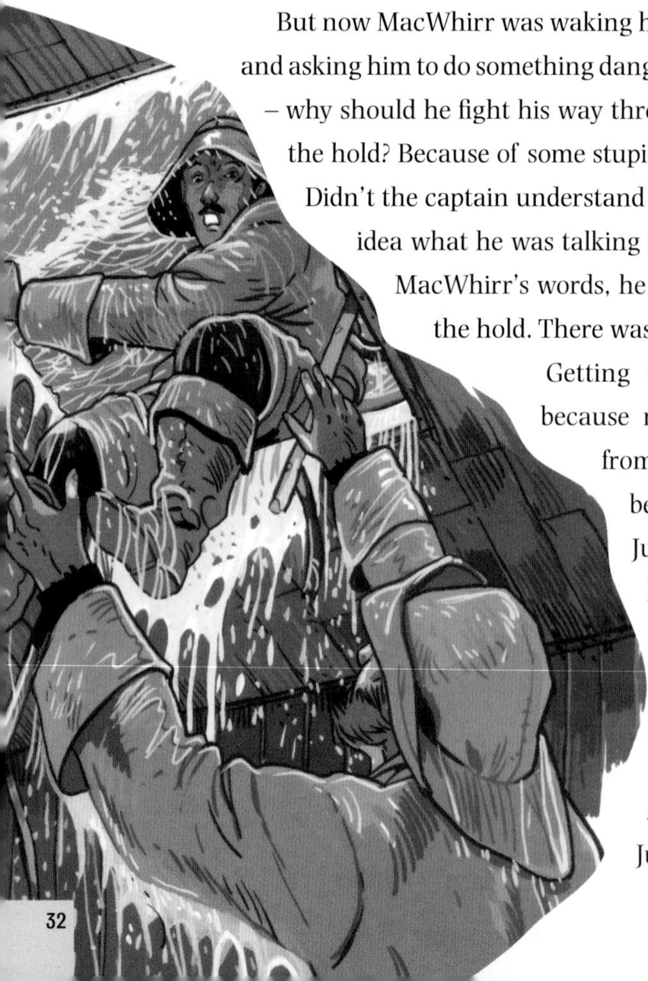

But now MacWhirr was waking him from this numb feeling, and asking him to do something dangerous. At first he felt angry – why should he fight his way through the typhoon down to the hold? Because of some stupid story of the boatswain's? Didn't the captain understand that the boatswain had no idea what he was talking about? But when he heard MacWhirr's words, he knew that he had to go to the hold. There was no way to avoid it.

Getting there was very difficult, because now there was no ladder from the bridge to the deck below. The boatswain held Jukes by the arms and helped him to climb down slowly onto the deck. Enormous waves were still hitting the ship, and twice they nearly went overboard. At last they got to the hold. Just when Jukes started to open the heavy door, the boatswain grabbed him by the arm.

'Be careful, sir. The wooden boxes are in pieces, and the money's all over the place. If those Chinese men think that you've come to take their money, it can easily turn dangerous.'

Jukes looked inside, afraid of what he would see. The hold had a lot of water in it. Just as the boatswain said, the money was all over the place. The Chinese labourers were going from one side of the hold to the other with each wave. Some of them were trying to climb a ladder that went up to a **hatch**. The ones at the top were hitting the hatch with their hands as hard as they could, but they couldn't open it. The ship started rolling the other way, and all the men on the ladder fell off slowly, one by one. Each one screamed as he hit the deck below. Some fell on top of the others. Then a really enormous wave lifted the ship right up, and all the men started rolling nearer the door of the hold, where the boatswain and Jukes were standing. A great wave of water, heads, legs and arms came their way. Jukes and the boatswain quickly ran out of the hold, and shut the door behind them. He looked at the boatswain, and saw the **horror** on his face. Was this how his face looked too? He had no idea what to do, or if there was anything that he could do. He just had to tell MacWhirr about it.

At the same time, MacWhirr decided to go to the wheelhouse. He had to see that everything was all right in this part of the ship. If there was a problem with the **rudder**, then there was no hope of surviving the typhoon. Like Jukes and the boatswain, he found it very difficult to move around the ship. The wind pulled at everything that he was wearing, and when he got to the wheelhouse, he found that his rainhat was gone from off his head. This made him angry. It was worse for him than losing the lifeboats.

hatch a little door in the ceiling

horror the feeling of being badly surprised and afraid

rudder the part of a ship in the water that changes the ship's direction

Inside the wheelhouse, he found the second mate sitting on the floor, his head in his hands. 'What are you doing here?' asked MacWhirr.

'It was my turn below deck,' cried the man. 'So I came in here some time back. You can't stop me!'

The captain looked up at the wheelhouse clock. It was half past one in the morning. 'A new day,' he said to himself.

'You'll never see the sun come up!' cried the second mate.

The captain said nothing back to him, but turned now to the **helmsman**. He was a sailor by the name of Hackett. He stood at the wheel, fighting to make sure that the ship stayed on course.

'He's a good man, to be working like that in weather like this for hour after hour,' thought MacWhirr.

'Is the rudder still all right?' asked the captain.

'Yes, sir,' answered Hackett.

'I want you to stay at the wheel. I can't send another man to take your place here. He won't know how to **control** the ship as well as you. Do you think you can go on without any rest?'

'Sir, I can **steer** her all day and all night if no one talks to me,' answered the helmsman.

'Erm ... I see ... yes, of course. Very good ... Hackett,' said MacWhirr. The helmsman's answer surprised him.

The captain went to the speaking-tube that they used to talk with the engine room. He called into it: 'Rout?'

He needed to see that the men in the engine room were making enough steam. This was another important part of trying to control the ship. He spoke loudly into the mouth of the speaking-tube again: 'Rout! Are you there?'

By putting his ear very close to the speaking-tube, he could just hear Rout's answer: 'I hear you, sir. It's not too good down here, but we're doing what we can. One of the engineers is hurt, but we're still making steam. How is it up above deck?'

'This typhoon is really pushing us about,' answered MacWhirr looking down at the second mate, who was still sitting on the floor. 'Rout, just make sure that we have enough steam.'

'Sir, we can't give the ship too much power. We may send her down *into* the waves, instead of *up and over* them.'

'I know, Rout, but we need enough power to steer. If we don't have that, we'll lose control of the ship – and then we'll sink.'

helmsman the person who stands at the ship's wheel and changes a ship's direction

control to make people or things do what you want

steer to move a boat or ship left or right

'So the wheelhouse is still all right?' asked the chief engineer.

'For now, yes. Rout, I need to speak to Jukes. Is he there? I want him to finish down in the hold and come up and help me. I'm alone here. The second mate has ...'

'Gone overboard?'

'No. He's lost his head.'

For some minutes the captain's voice was silent, but Rout could hear the noise of a fight coming down the speaking tube. At last, the captain came back.

'The second mate ran at me. He isn't well. I had to knock him on the head. Did you hear?'

Rout went off to see to the engines, but as soon as Jukes arrived in the engine room, the chief engineer pushed him over to the speaking-tubes to talk to MacWhirr.

'I went to look at the Chinese labourers, sir. And from what I saw, this is what happened: at first the typhoon made them afraid, and quiet. Then one of the boxes fell onto the floor of the hold and broke. When they saw the money on the floor, some tried to grab it. That started a fight. With the rolling of the ship, they went from one side of the hold to the other, and the others **joined** the fight. Now the storm has broken all the boxes, and all of them are fighting over all of the money. I don't see how we can stop it now, sir. I think that some are dead, and it seems that many are hurt.'

Jukes hoped that Captain MacWhirr wouldn't give him any more to do in the hold. Then the captain's answer came down the speaking-tube:

'Get some men and go back to the hold. **Pick up** all the money and put it somewhere safe. Typhoon or no typhoon I don't want any fighting on the *Nan-Shan* ...'

join to do something that other people are already doing; to put things together

pick up to take something in your hand

'I have to pick up the labourers' money in the hold,' said Jukes to Rout on his way out of the engine room.

'What?!' replied the chief engineer. 'First the second mate goes and hits the captain, now you're making the hold tidy. Haven't you officers got anything better to do?'

Down in the engine room, in the deepest part of the ship, they couldn't see the enormous wall of dark sea water that was just going to hit the *Nan-Shan*.

ACTIVITIES

READING CHECK

Who says these words?

1 If those Chinese men think that you've come to take their money, it can easily turn dangerous.

2 You'll never see the sun come up.

3 The second mate ran at me. He isn't well. I had to knock him on the head.

4 Typhoon or no typhoon, I don't want any fighting on the *Nan-Shan*.

5 I can steer her all day and night if no one talks to me.

6 Haven't you officers got anything better to do?

7 I think that some are dead, and it seems that many are hurt.

8 I have to pick up the labourers' money in the hold.

a ...3... says MacWhirr to Rout.
b .... says Jukes to MacWhirr.
c .... says MacWhirr to Jukes.
d .... says the boatswain to Jukes.
e .... says Jukes to Rout.
f .... says Rout to Jukes.
g .... says Hackett to MacWhirr.
h .... says the second mate to MacWhirr.

WORD WORK

1 These words don't match the pictures. Correct them.

~~ladder~~
rudder

wheelhouse

rudder

helmsman

hatch

2 Complete these sentences with the correct form of the words around the ship's wheel.

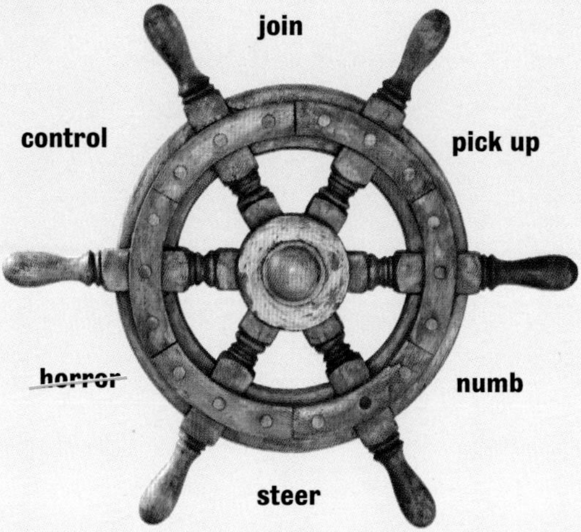

a We watched with ...horror... as the ship slowly sank. It was a terrible accident!

b My hand is going .... I can't feel my fingers any more.

c When he was still a young man, he .... the crew of a ship that was sailing for South America.

d It's very difficult to .... a ship well in a storm. The wind and the waves push you off course.

e The rudder is broken, and the engines have no power: we've lost .... of the ship. The sea will take it here and there and we can't do anything about it!

f Can you .... your things from the floor? You're very untidy.

GUESS WHAT

What happens in the next chapter? Match the two halves of each sentence.

a MacWhirr	**1** climbs the enormous wave.
b Jukes	**2** go with Jukes to help him.
c The centre of the typhoon	**3** points to 'Very Stormy'.
d The *Nan-Shan*	**4** says that the typhoon will get worse.
e The barometer	**5** is less windy.
f Some of the crew	**6** goes to pick up the Chinese labourers' money.

Chapter 7 The storm in the hold

The dark wave that came quickly nearer and nearer to the *Nan-Shan* looked as high as a mountain, and had a thin white line up at the top of it. The ship was still for a while, and then she started to climb this mountain of water. **Tons** of water fell onto the deck. Every man on the ship grabbed what he could, and held on. The *Nan-Shan* climbed the enormous wave for what seemed like a very long time. Then she began to go down the other side. Again, tons of water fell heavily onto the ship, making her shake from top to bottom.

In the engine room, Jukes and Rout looked at each other with horror on their faces.

'If another wave like that hits us, it'll finish us,' said Rout.

'What can be left on deck after such an enormous wave? If it **destroyed** the ventilators, there's no hope. Now it's all gone up there for sure – the wheelhouse, the bridge, the chart-room – everything,' said Jukes.

But there was no second wave, and a short while later they heard MacWhirr's voice in the speaking-tube again:

'That was a little uncomfortable. But we have to do our best. Jukes, when your men have picked up all the money, I want you to come back up to the bridge. I need you here.'

tons lots and lots of something

destroy to break every part of something or someone

'Yes, sir,' replied Jukes, and – not feeling very happy about it – he went to get some men for the job.

Twenty minutes later, Jukes and sixteen of the crew arrived at the hold. Opening the door for the second time, he saw the same **chaos** as before. But this time he was ready for it. Shouting at his men to help, he started to push the Chinese labourers into one corner of the room. The crew joined arms to make them all stay in the same place. One of the crew then brought some **rope**, and they used this to make **lifelines**. Now the Chinese labourers could grab onto the lifelines, and not fall from side to side. After they fastened the ropes well to the sides of the hold, Jukes and his men started to move all the broken pieces of wood and the money into a locked room just next to the hold.

chaos something which is out of control

rope a very thick, strong string

lifelines ropes that people can hold onto in a storm

While Jukes and his men were doing this work, the Chinese labourers were terrified. What did these sailors want to do to them? Some thought that they were going to steal all their money. Others thought that Jukes and his men were there to kill them.

They sat on the floor, their faces full of fear. But to Jukes their fear looked like fury. Suddenly one of the labourers started speaking to him loudly in Chinese. He pointed at the locked room where their money was, and then started shouting. At once, the rest of them started shouting at Jukes and the crew. The crew didn't understand them, but their Chinese words seemed angry, and they seemed to be **threatening** Jukes and the others. So Jukes and the rest of the crew left the hold as quickly as possible, closing the heavy metal door behind them loudly.

They were all happy to be out of the hold. It was not only because of the Chinese labourers there; sailors don't like the idea of drowning below the deck.

At once, Jukes went up to the bridge to look for MacWhirr. He found him there, holding on to the railings.

'We did it, sir. We picked up all the money like you said, and we fastened some lifelines to the walls for the Chinese labourers to hold on to.'

'Well done. I knew that you could do it,' answered MacWhirr.

'Did you?' said Jukes to himself.

'The wind's stopped,' said MacWhirr.

It was true. Although the waves were still enormous, there was no wind at all. Suddenly Jukes noted that he could again hear all the usual noises of the ship – the deep noise of the engines, the crew calling out to each other, the noise of **creaking** wood.

'It's not over yet. My book says that there's worse still to

threaten to say that you will do something bad to someone to make them feel afraid

creaking a noise that wood makes in a ship or a house

come,' explained MacWhirr. The *Nan-Shan* was now in the eye of the storm, the **exact** centre of it – where all was strangely quiet and **calm**. Soon they would start sailing through the other part of the storm.

exact true; no more nor less than

calm not moving; not worried

But Jukes seemed not to hear what MacWhirr was saying. He went on, 'It wasn't easy. We had to fight to do the job. They didn't understand that we were trying to help them. They seemed to think that we were trying to hurt them. I was worried when we put all their money in the locked room. They didn't like that at all. They started to shout at us. I think that they were threatening us. We had to get out of there as quickly as possible. You told me to pick up all the money, but it wasn't as easy as it seems.'

'Well, we had to do the right thing by those labourers, Jukes. Even if we have only five minutes more to live, we've done the right thing by them. And that's that.'

Jukes was still excited about his adventure, and had more to say.

'But that isn't the end of it, sir. They're quiet now, but there's going to be more trouble. They know that this isn't a British ship any more. I didn't like that Thai flag from the start, sir. And it's not going to be easy when we give them back their money.'

'No, this isn't the end of it,' answered MacWhirr. 'Can you stay on deck for a minute, Jukes?'

'Are you going below, sir?' asked Jukes quickly. From his voice it seemed he felt sure that the storm would start once he was alone on the bridge and in command of the ship.

The captain went into the chart-room. It was dark inside, but he knew the room well, and felt his way. He lit one of the lamps and went over to look at the barometer. It was pointing down to 'Very Stormy' – the worst MacWhirr had ever seen. So the book that he was reading and the barometer agreed, getting out of the typhoon would be far worse than getting into it. He looked around the room that was usually so tidy but was now in chaos, and thought, 'Perhaps it's the last time I'll do this!'

'I got another man to take Hackett's place,' said Jukes to the captain when MacWhirr came out on deck again. 'It wasn't easy to get anyone to do it, but I didn't want to have to be helmsman myself. Hackett's resting now, not far from the wheel. He looks half dead. The second mate's there, too. Is he hurt, sir?'

'No. He isn't right in the head.'

'But he's hit himself, sir. He's got a cut on the side of his face.'

'Yes. I had to knock him down. Listen, Jukes, the typhoon will come back very soon, and this time it'll be worse than before. It'll take this ship and pick her up, and shake her and try to break her. It'll take what's still above deck. Of course I know that there's not much now to take ...'

'... only us two,' said Jukes.

'Yes, and if the typhoon takes me, you'll be in command. The second mate will be no help to you,' answered MacWhirr. Jukes was suddenly quiet at this. MacWhirr went on: 'If that happens, make sure that you go on sailing into the wind, do you hear? Stay on course, and stay calm. Hold that one idea in your head, and the ship will survive.'

Just then, they could hear the noise of the wind again. It seemed like a great number of soldiers hurrying nearer very fast. The few minutes of calm were finished. MacWhirr thought for a minute about how well he knew the *Nan-Shan* from years of sailing her. She was almost like a home for him. 'I wouldn't like to lose her,' he said aloud to himself, while the waves began to hit the deck again.

ACTIVITIES

READING CHECK

Match the pictures with the sentences.

1 Jukes

2 the *Nan-Shan*

3 the Chinese labourers

4 Hackett

5 the second mate

6 the crew

7 Rout

8 MacWhirr

a ...7..... says that the ship won't survive another enormous wave.

b .... has got a cut on his head because MacWhirr knocked him down.

c .... climbs the enormous wave and goes down the other side.

d The second time .... is ready for the chaos in the hold.

e .... think that the crew have come to kill them or steal all their money.

f .... leave the hold as quickly as they can.

g Jukes finds another man to take the place of .... at the wheel.

h .... tells Jukes that Jukes will be in command if anything happens to him.

WORD WORK

Complete Jukes's letter on page 17 with the correct form of the words around the picture.

ACTIVITIES

There was so much water on deck – a) ...tons...... *of it! One more wave like that would kill us all and* b) .... *the ventilators. And I still had to go to the hold to pick up all the money. When the crew and I got there, it was* c) .... *: there was money all over the deck, broken pieces of wood lay everywhere, and the Chinese labourers were screaming and shouting. But this time I knew what to do. We got the* d) .... *and used it to make* e) .... *for the Chinese to hold onto. Then we picked up all the money, put it in a room next to the hold, and locked it to avoid trouble. I don't know why, but the Chinese looked terrified. We weren't* f) .... *them, in fact we were only trying to help, but one of them started shouting, and then suddenly all of them were shouting at us! We left as fast as we could. Then, while I was telling the captain about it, the wind stopped – suddenly it was* g) .... *. We were in the eye of the storm, the* h) .... *centre of the typhoon. I have never known a stranger moment at sea. It didn't last long, but there was more to come...*

GUESS WHAT

What happens in the next chapter? Tick the boxes.

a The *Nan-Shan*
- sinks in the typhoon. ☐
- survives the typhoon. ☐

b The *Nan-Shan* is
- ready for another journey. ☐
- not ready for another journey. ☐

c The second mate
- leaves the ship. ☐
- stays with the ship. ☐

d MacWhirr
- keeps all the Chinese labourers' money. ☐
- gives all the money back to the Chinese labourers. ☐

e The Chinese labourers
- take their money calmly. ☐
- all fight over their money. ☐

f MacWhirr wants to go on shore to
- have a nice, cold drink. ☐
- buy some more pens and pencils. ☐

g Mrs MacWhirr
- wants to see more of her husband. ☐
- doesn't want to see more of her husband. ☐

CHAPTER 8 Three letters

The *Nan-Shan* arrived in Fu-chau on a bright, sunny day. She looked a real **sight**, and soon everyone in the **harbour** was talking about her.

'That ship looks like she's just come back from a **war**,' said one.

'It looks to me like the crew found her at the bottom of the sea and pulled her up to sell her for the metal,' said another.

'I'll buy her – for five pounds!' said a third.

Less than an hour after MacWhirr's ship arrived, a small boat took a thin man with an angry red face off the ship, and left him on shore. While the boat moved away, the thin man turned and shook his hand angrily at the *Nan-Shan*. A tall fat sailor with watery eyes came over to speak to the man, who was no longer the *Nan Shan*'s second mate.

sight something that you see

harbour a place where ships can stop safely near land

war fighting between countries

'Hello, old friend!'

'Hello, there. What are you doing here?' said the thin man, quickly shaking hands.

'I heard that perhaps there's a job going,' said the fat man.

The one-time second mate shook his hand angrily at the *Nan-Shan* again.

'I wouldn't let the captain of that ship be in command of the poorest river boat!' he cried angrily.

'Really?' said his fat friend.

'Of course, I'd like to make trouble for him. But he's sailing under a Thai flag. What can I do? You know, he told his chief engineer that I wasn't right in the head. Me! He's the stupidest man that ever sailed the seas! You can't really be thinking of ...'

'Did you get your money?' asked his fat friend suddenly.

'Oh, yes. He paid me before I left. "Have your breakfast on shore!" he told me.'

'Did he? Shall we go and have a drink then?'

'And he hit me.'

'He didn't! You must tell me all about it. But not here. I know a quiet place where we can have a bottle or two of something nice and cold.'

And so the two of them walked away together into town.

Jukes watched them go, and then went back to planning the **repairs** that the poor old *Nan-Shan* needed. She was no longer the beautiful ship that sailed out of Dumbarton just three years before. She looked old and tired, like an enormous animal that has won a great fight against a terrible enemy, a fight which has broken it inside. While Jukes was speaking to the crew, telling them what to do, Captain MacWhirr stood on the bridge, looking

repairs when you make things that are broken work again

at the harbour and at the town behind it. He was thinking about what he would need to buy in Fu-chau. His pens and pencils all went overboard during the typhoon, and he would need to get new ones. And he needed a new rainhat, too. He was happy to survive the typhoon, but he did not think about that much now. Perhaps the only thing that the typhoon really did was to take this quiet man, shake him up a little, and make him speak a few more words than usual.

Back in England not long after that, three people were reading three letters. The first, Mrs MacWhirr, was reading her letter in the same way that she read all her husband's letters. She read a few words here and there, to get an idea of more or less what it was about. *'They are called typhoons ... Jukes didn't seem to like it ... some things that you can't find in books ...'* Why were his letters always so long and full of **details**? *'A calm that lasted for more than twenty minutes ... see you and the children again ...'* Now why did he say that? He was always thinking of coming home! What need was there for that when he had such a good job? Worriedly, she quickly went on a few pages: *'... only three with broken*

detail a small piece of information

legs ... the ***fairest*** *way ... tried to do the right thing ...'* No, there was no more about coming home. Reading so quickly, she didn't see the part that said: *'For a while I thought that I would never see you and the children again.'* The door opened and Lydia, her daughter, ran into the room. Seeing the letter in her mother's hand, she stopped in surprise, and waited to hear the latest news.

'Your father's well,' said Mrs MacWhirr. Lydia did not look very interested.

'Go and get your hat,' said her mother. 'We're going out: there's a **sale** at Linom's, that shop which you like so much.'

'How wonderful!' shouted Lydia, and she ran to get her hat.

Outside Linom's, Mrs MacWhirr saw one of her friends. They talked about shops, clothes – and their husbands.

'No, he's not coming home yet. It's terrible that he has to be away from us for so long, but it's good to know that he's well. He likes the weather in the China Sea.' From the way that she talked, it seemed that poor Captain MacWhirr only sailed to China because of his **health**.

Mrs Rout was reading out her husband's letter to Rout's mother: *'The captain of the ship did something very clever. It's difficult to explain how clever it really was.* Do you remember Captain MacWhirr? Solomon said that he wasn't the quickest thinker.'

Young Mrs Rout turned the pages to find out what this clever thing was. But she could find nothing.

'Oh no ... I don't understand.'

'What don't you understand, dear?' asked old Mrs Rout. She liked her son's letters, although she couldn't remember very well what he looked like. It was a very long time since she last saw him.

fair good for all people

sale when you can buy things in a shop for less than usual

health how well and strong people are

'Well, there's nothing more about this clever thing that the captain did. Why doesn't he tell us more about it?'

'I don't know my dear,' said old Mrs Rout.

But the last part of the letter the younger Mrs Rout read silently to herself: *'I know that we can't do anything at the moment because of my mother. But I want you to come out here. I'd like to buy you a small house where we could see each other. We spend so little time together, and we're not getting any younger.'*

Young Mrs Rout was quiet for a while, and she looked unhappy. Then she shook herself, and said to old Mrs Rout: 'He's well, the same as always. Come on, let's have a cup of tea.'

Jukes's letter to his friend gave all the details of the 'clever thing' that Captain MacWhirr did. First, he wrote all about the typhoon, and then about how he and the crew made lifelines for the Chinese labourers in the hold.

'The problems started when we picked up all their money. They thought that we were trying to steal it. Only very desperate **robbers** *could think of stealing money in the middle of a typhoon! Some of them even started shouting at us. When I spoke to the captain, I said that we should be careful when we were giving the money back. I said that all the crew should be there and that we should have some guns with us. That way there would be no problems. He didn't seem to like my idea. Well, we had a lot of repairs to do after the typhoon, and I made the men start working on them. I was very tired after nearly thirty hours without sleep, so I went to lie down on my bed for a while.*

Some time later one of the crew woke me. He told me that the Chinese labourers were all on deck and that MacWhirr was giving them their money. I couldn't believe it. I called some of the crew, we got the guns, and we ran there as quickly as possible. When MacWhirr

robber a person who takes something that is not theirs from a place

saw me, he was really angry, and he told me to put the guns away. It seems that, while I was sleeping, he decided – because all the labourers were seven-year ones – that the fairest thing was to give each labourer exactly the same ***amount*** *of money. One of the Chinese labourers helped to explain this to the others. And so MacWhirr gave each man his money, while all the others waited their turn. Then he gave the* ***injured*** *labourers their money. In the end there was a little extra money, and he gave this to the ones who were the most injured.*

For a man who's always so slow and sure, I must say that he did very well.'

amount the number of things like coins

injured badly hurt

READING CHECK

Are these sentences true or false? Tick the boxes.

	True	False
a The *Nan-Shan* looks as beautiful as when she was first built.	☐	☑
b The second mate is angry with MacWhirr.	☐	☐
c The typhoon has not really changed MacWhirr very much.	☐	☐
d MacWhirr doesn't give many details in his letter to his wife.	☐	☐
e Mrs MacWhirr hopes that her husband will come back to England.	☐	☐
f Mrs Rout misses her husband.	☐	☐
g There were many problems when MacWhirr gave the Chinese back their money.	☐	☐
h Both Rout and Jukes think that MacWhirr was cleverer than usual with the Chinese labourers' money.	☐	☐

WORD WORK

Complete each sentence with the correct pair of words.

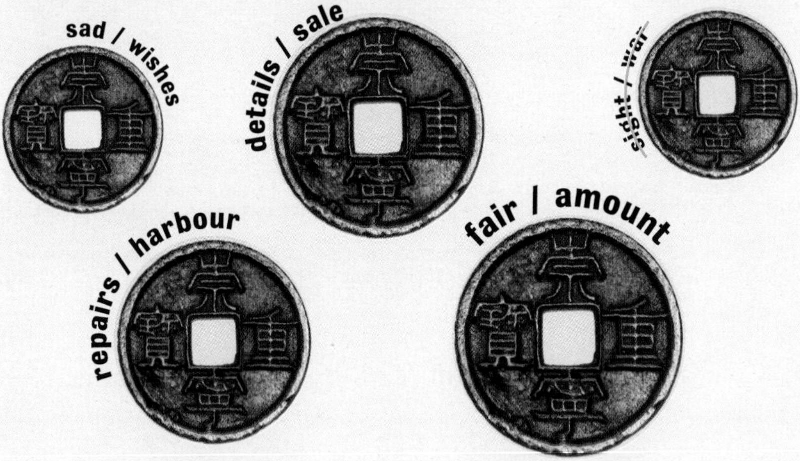

a When the *Nan-Shan* arrives in Fu-chau, she's a terrible ......sight...... and people say that she looks like she's just come back from a ......war...... .

b The *Nan-Shan* needs to have many .... while she's in .... in Fu-chau.

c To be ...., MacWhirr gives each Chinese labourer exactly the same .... of money.

d Mrs MacWhirr doesn't find the .... of her husband's letter interesting, and she decides to take her daughter to a .... in her favourite shop.

e Mrs Rout is .... because she sees her husband so little, and she .... that she could be with him more.

GUESS WHAT

What happens after the story ends? Choose from these ideas, or add your own.

a The owners of the *Nan-Shan* are angry that MacWhirr didn't try to avoid the typhoon.

b The owners of the *Nan-Shan* are happy that the ship and all the people on her survived.

c MacWhirr decides to leave his job and go back to his family in England.

d MacWhirr commands ships in the China Sea for many more years.

e After repairs the *Nan-Shan* sails again, but never meets another typhoon.

f Rout's mother dies, and his wife comes to live in a little house on the coast of China.

g Jukes moves to another ship, and after a few years is made a captain.

Project A *Writing cinquains*

1 A cinquain is a poem in five lines.

Read the poem above, and answer the questions about the rules of writing this kind of cinquain:

- **a** How many syllables are there in line 1, and in line 5?
- **b** How many syllables are there in lines 2, 3 and 4?
- **c** Which lines tell us the subject of the poem?
- **d** Which line describes this person?
- **e** Which line tells us what he does?
- **f** Which line tells us some more information about MacWhirr?

2 Look at this cinquain about Mr Rout. (The lines are in the wrong order, and each line has an extra syllable.)

a Take away a one-syllable word from each line.

b Put the lines in the correct order. (Number them 1–5)

Likes working, talking, loving.	☐
Smiling, and gentle;	☐
Nice Old Rout:	☐
Wants to spend lots more time with his wife.	☐
A good man!	☐

3 Choose another character in one of the chapters in *Typhoon* and write a cinquain about him or her. Follow the rules in Activity 1.

Project B *Writing a report*

The *Nan-Shan*'s owners want to know what happened before, during, and after the typhoon. They interview crew members and take notes. Then they write a report.

1 Read the notes. Which key event are they describing? Write it in the notes.

a) the beginning of the typhoon b) visiting the hold c) the end of the typhoon

Interview with: Mr Jukes, the first mate

Key event: ....

What did he see?

The waves became very big.
The barometer showed that the weather would be bad.
The wind became very strong.

What did he feel?

worried
a little afraid
surprised that Captain MacWhirr said nothing

What did he do?

He wrote in the logbook.
He looked at the sky and the sea.
He saw the swell.
He went to speak with Captain MacWhirr.

What did he say?

'The swell's getting worse.'
'A lot of water is coming into the ship's hold.'
'I thought that we could go east.'

2 Use the notes to complete the parts of the report here and at the top of page 59. Each gap can contain one or more words.

Report on the beginning of the storm

The first mate, Mr Jukes, saw that the weather was changing, and the *barometer* showed that there was bad weather coming. The .... became very strong, and the .... became very big.

The first mate was worried and he felt .... He didn't understand why .... said nothing. The captain seemed very relaxed: just before the storm, he had a sleep.

After looking at the ...., Jukes wrote about the weather every night in .... Looking at ...., Jukes saw that it was getting worse. He decided to .... Captain MacWhirr.

When Jukes spoke to the captain, he told MacWhirr that .... was coming into the hold. Jukes said that the Chinese would be more comfortable if they ...., away from the storm. The captain thought that was very funny. MacWhirr told Jukes that a ship just had to go through any kind of weather. He said that they were not going to change direction.

3 Put each word or phrase into the correct part of the form below.

'They are all fighting over the money.'

fear

He looked inside the hold.

on't see how we can stop it now.'

Jukes

money all over the deck

the Chinese labourers going from side to side

horror

He left the hold and quickly shut the door again.

Who? ....

Key event: Jukes and the boatswain go to see what has really happened in the hold.

What did he see?
a lot of water inside the hold
....
....

What did he feel?
worried that the Chinese labourers were thinking that he wanted to take their money
....
....

What did he do?
....
....
He went to the engine room to tell MacWhirr about the Chinese labourers in the hold.

What did he say?
'I went to look at the Chinese labourers.'
....
....

4 Complete the report with information from the form.

Report on...

The first mate saw...

Mr Jukes felt...

Jukes decided...

He spoke to...

5 Imagine an interview with a different character about a different key event in the story. Write notes on the form.

Who? ....

Key event: ....

What did he see?
....
....
....

What did he feel?
....
....
....

What did he do?
....
....
....

What did he say?
....
....
....

6 Write a report from your notes.

GRAMMAR

GRAMMAR CHECK

Past Simple: affirmative

We use the Past Simple to talk about finished actions that happened in the past.

With regular verbs we usually add –ed/–d to the infinitive form.

The enormous wave crashed onto the deck. *The ship arrived at last.*

With regular verbs that end in consonant + –y we change y to i and add –ed.

marry – MacWhirr married Lucy after he became a captain.

Many verbs are irregular. You must learn their past forms.

run – MacWhirr ran away from home when he was 15.

1 Complete the sentences with the Past Simple form of the verbs in brackets.

a They ...arrived... (arrive) in Fu-chau.

b The *Nan-Shan* .... (sail) into the eye of the storm.

c MacWhirr, Jukes, and Rout all .... (send) new letters home.

d Jukes .... (go) to the chart-room to write the ship's log.

e The boatswain .... (say) that all the Chinese labourers were in the sea.

f MacWhirr, Jukes, and Rout .... (write) letters before the start of the journey.

g Jukes and the boatswain .... (fight) their way to the hold to see what was happening.

h MacWhirr .... (give) the Chinese labourers their money.

i Jukes and his men .... (tie) lifelines from one side of the hold to the other.

j The typhoon .... (start) later that evening.

k The second engineer .... (want) to move one of the ventilators.

l Everybody .... (feel) very hot on the first afternoon.

m They .... (pick up) all the money and .... (put) it in a locked room.

n The second mate .... (leave) the ship.

o Jukes .... (talk) about the new Thai flag with Rout.

2 Now put the sentences in the order that they happen in the story.

o Jukes talked about the new Thai flag with Rout.

GRAMMAR CHECK

Infinitive of purpose

We can use the infinitive to explain why we do something.

Jukes went to the hold to check on the Chinese labourers.

3 Complete these sentences about the story using the verbs in the box. Some verbs can be used in more than one sentence.

learn	see	make	check	have	~~write~~	keep	stop	talk

a Jukes went to his cabin to to write a letter to his friend.

b Captain MacWhirr looked at the barometer .... what kind of weather was coming.

c The Chinese labourers were washing themselves in sea water .... cool.

d MacWhirr was reading a book .... more about typhoons.

e Harry the second engineer came up on deck .... one of the ventilators.

f Jukes went to the chart-room .... about the storm with MacWhirr.

g MacWhirr sat down on his sofa .... a short rest.

h The sailors grabbed the railings .... themselves going into the sea.

i MacWhirr put his arm around Jukes's shoulders .... him feel less afraid.

4 Match these questions with the correct answers.

a Why did Jukes want to change course?

b Why did the boatswain leave the crew?

c Why did MacWhirr go to the wheelhouse?

d Why did Jukes and his men tie ropes from one side of the hold to the other?

e Why did Jukes and his men put all the money in a locked room?

f Why did MacWhirr want to see all the Chinese labourers in Fu-chau?

1 To keep it safe.

2 To find a light.

3 To avoid the typhoon.

4 To give back their money.

5 To give the Chinese labourers something to hold onto.

6 To check that the steering was still working.

GRAMMAR CHECK

Talking about the future

We use will, going to, and the Present Continuous to talk about the future.

When we think about a plan before we speak, we use going to or the Present Continuous.

'I'm going to pick up the Chinese labourers' money.'

We're sailing for Fu-chau this afternoon.

We often use the Present Continuous to talk about things in the future that are *already organized*.

We use will to talk about decisions we make *at the moment* of speaking.

'I'll buy her for five pounds!' said a sailor when he saw the Nan-Shan.

5 These sentences show what different characters might say or think at different times in the story. Complete them using the correct form of the verb in brackets – *going to*, *will*, or the *Present Continuous*.

a 'I don't like that Thai flag. I ...'m going to speak / 'll speak..... (speak) to Captain MacWhirr about it,' said Jukes.

b 'Captain MacWhirr: on Friday 8th September you .... (sail) the *Nan-Shan* to Fu-chau, with two hundred Chinese labourers on board,' said Mr Sigg.

c 'I .... (speak) to Jukes about those ventilators. I don't know why they aren't working,' said Harry.

d 'We .... (spend) Christmas in Hong Kong. Then we .... (leave) for Macau on the 27th December,' wrote MacWhirr to his parents.

e 'Go and tell the Chinese labourers to come up on deck,' said Captain MacWhirr to one of the crew. 'I .... (give) them their money in exactly fifteen minutes.'

f 'I .... (check) the wheelhouse, and see if everything is all right,' said MacWhirr.

g 'The Chinese labourers .... (arrive) very soon. Show them where to go,' said MacWhirr to Jukes.

h 'I .... (meet) the captain of a Portuguese ship at three o'clock this afternoon, to talk about a job. Why don't you come too?' said the fat sailor to the ex-second mate of the *Nan-Shan*.

GRAMMAR CHECK

Verbs of perception

We use the verbs feel, look, and sound with an adjective to describe something using our senses.

The wind of the typhoon sounded very frightening.

6 Complete these sentences with *felt*, *looked*, and *sounded*.

a The Thai flag ..looked.. very strange to Jukes.

b Before the storm, the air .... thick and heavy.

c Old Rout's voice .... very weak through the speaking-tube.

d When Jukes went into the hold, the Chinese labourers .... very frightened.

e The labourers shouted in Chinese and pointed at the locked room. Their voices .... angry.

f The clouds hid the stars and the sky .... very dark.

g The rain on MacWhirr's face .... very cold.

h When the *Nan-Shan* arrived in Fu-chau, she .... old and tired.

7 Write short answers to these questions, using *feel*, *look*, and *sound* with an adjective.

a How did Mrs Rout look when she read her husband's second letter?

She looked sad.

b What did the wind sound like?

....

c What did the ship feel like during the storm?

....

d How did Mrs MacWhirr sound when she told her daughter Lydia about her father's letter?

....

e How did Lydia look when she heard they were going to the shop?

....

GRAMMAR CHECK

Echo questions

When we want to check what we have heard, or show surprise or interest, we use short questions which 'echo' the subject and the auxiliary verb.

'We're sailing towards a typhoon.' *'Are we?'*

'I can see an enormous wave above us.' *'Can you?'*

In the Present Simple or Past Simple, with verbs apart from *be*, *have got*, *can*, and *could*, we use do or did.

'MacWhirr always wears the same brown suit when he's on shore.' *'Does he?'*

'The waves took all the ship's lifeboats.' *'Did they?'*

8 Match Captain MacWhirr's 'echo questions' in the box with what Jukes says.

Could we?	Has it?	~~Is it?~~	Won't she?	Are they?
Were you?	Did they?	Do I?	Don't you?	Are you?

a The swell's getting worse, Captain MacWhirr. Is it?

b I'm very worried about the weather, sir. ....

c I was thinking about the ship's course. ....

d You need to hear what I think about this. ....

e We could try and avoid the storm. ....

f The Chinese said it's going to be a typhoon. ....

g I don't think that we should sail through it. ....

h The *Nan-Shan* won't survive a typhoon. ....

i The wind has been like this for the last half hour. ....

j The waves are getting bigger and bigger. ....

9 Now write Jukes's 'echo questions' for MacWhirr's sentences.

a I was just reading about storms in this book. Were you?

b The book says that we should sail all over the sea to avoid a storm. ....

c I think that's a stupid idea. ....

d It will take us two more days to get to Fu-chau. ....

e They won't be happy about that. ....

f A typhoon is just a little bad weather. ....

g We must sail straight through it. ....

GRAMMAR CHECK

Conditional sentences

We use 'if' to talk about what will happen in a possible situation in different ways. Here are two examples:

1 **'if' clause + imperative main clause**

This is telling someone what to do.

Jukes, if I die in the typhoon, take command of the ship.

2 **'if' clause + Present Simple + 'will' future main clause**

This is saying what the result will be.

If you don't calm down, second mate, I'll hit you.

10 Match the two parts of the sentences correctly.

a If we tie these ropes from one wall to the other,	**1** the ship will break in two.
b If you have to take command of the ship,	**2** tell me what you have done.
c If we get another wave like that,	**3** we won't be able to steer.
d If the ship loses power,	**4** we'll need a rest in Fu-chau.
e If the ship has too much power,	**5** the Chinese will have something to hold onto.
f If you can get to the speaking-tube,	**6** make sure you go on sailing into the wind.
g If we survive this,	**7** she'll go into the waves, instead of over them.

11 Now complete these sentences with your own ideas.

a MacWhirr: If we don't pick up the Chinese labourers' money,

....

b Jukes: If the Chinese labourers make problems when we are giving the money back,

....

c MacWhirr: If the second mate tries to come back to the ship,

....

d Second mate: If I ever see Captain MacWhirr again,

....

GRAMMAR CHECK

Participle phrases

Sometimes we want to talk about two actions that happen at the same time.

'Did you leave your job?' asked Rout. He was smiling.

It is shorter, and more dramatic, to put a comma (,) after the first verb phrase and put the second verb in the –ing form just after this.

'Did you leave your job?' asked Rout, smiling.

12 Change the following pairs of sentences in the same way as above.

a 'It looks like bad weather out there,' thought MacWhirr. He was looking at the barometer.

It looks like bad weather out there, thought MacWhirr, looking at the barometer.

b 'She's a good ship, she'll take us through the typhoon,' said MacWhirr. He thought they would be lucky to survive.

....

c 'The captain wants me to go and pick up the Chinese labourers' money in the hold,' said Jukes. He looked angry.

....

d 'I can steer this ship all night,' said Hackett. He was fighting to control the wheel.

....

e The Chinese labourers fell from the ladder onto the deck. They screamed.

....

f The second mate was in the wheelhouse. He was sitting on the floor.

....

g One of the Chinese shouted at Jukes. He was pointing at the locked door.

....

h 'There's worse to come,' said MacWhirr. He looked up at a sky that was as black as coal.

....

i 'I shouldn't like to lose her,' thought MacWhirr. He remembered the many happy hours spent on the *Nan-Shan's* bridge.

....

DOMINOES Your Choice

Read *Dominoes* for pleasure, or to develop language skills. It's your choice.

Each *Domino* reader includes:
- a good story to enjoy
- integrated activities to develop reading skills and increase vocabulary
- task-based projects – perfect for CEFR portfolios
- contextualized grammar activities

Each *Domino* pack contains a reader, and an excitingly dramatized audio recording of the story

If you liked this *Domino*, read these:

The Lost World

Sir Arthur Conan Doyle

'You said that you wanted danger, didn't you?' says McArdle, the editor of the Daily Gazette. And he sends his young reporter, Malone, on a strange journey into South America with the famous Professor Challenger.

Challenger believes that he can find a lost world full of dinosaurs in the middle of the Amazon Forest. But this world is dangerous to reach, and, once the Professor and his small group of explorers arrive, things get even more dangerous for them.

Will they return alive?

Sherlock Holmes: The Norwood Mystery

Sir Arthur Conan Doyle

'For me, Watson, life is not so interesting,' says Holmes. 'I loved to read the newspaper, hoping to find some news of an interesting crime for me to investigate or a dangerous criminal for me to catch. Where are all those clever criminals these days?'

Then, suddenly, a wild, excited young man runs up the stairs to Holmes' room. He has a story to tell about a strange crime that took place in Norwood. But who is the criminal? And is he dangerous? Life, for Holmes, suddenly starts to get interesting.

	CEFR	Cambridge Exams	IELTS	TOEFL iBT	TOEIC
Level 3	B1	PET	4.0	57-86	550
Level 2	A2–B1	KET-PET	3.0-4.0	–	390
Level 1	A1–A2	YLE Flyers/KET	3.0	–	225
Starter & Quick Starter	A1	YLE Movers	1.0–2.0	–	–

You can find details and a full list of books and teachers' resources on our website:
www.oup.com/elt/gradedreaders